Tales From Shakespeare

A Complete Course in the Study of English

Spelling, Language, Grammar, Composition, Literature.

Reed's Word Lessons—A Complete Speller.
 Reed & Kellogg's Graded Lessons in English.
  Reed & Kellogg's Higher Lessons in English.
   Kellogg's Text-Book on Rhetoric.
    Kellogg's Text-Book on English Literature.

In the preparation of this series the authors have had one object clearly in view—to so develop the study of the English language as to present a complete, progressive course, from the Spelling-Book to the study of English Literature. The troublesome contradictions which arise in using books arranged by different authors on these subjects, and which require much time for explanation in the school-room, will be avoided by the use of the above "Complete Course."

Teachers are earnestly invited to examine these books.

CLARK & MAYNARD, Publishers,
771 Broadway, New York.

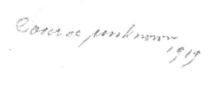

INTRODUCTION.

THE delightful little book, called *Tales from Shakespeare,* and published more than seventy-five years ago, was written by a brother and his sister, Charles and Mary Lamb. Their personal and literary lives are of singular interest and of the sweetest and gentlest heroism. Mary Lamb, the sister, was eleven years older than her brother, having been born in 1764. Charles Lamb, the brother, the genial essayist and critic, was born in London in 1775. His parents were in humble station, but managed to give their son a fair education. At the age of seven, he entered the school of Christ Hospital, where he remained till he was fourteen. Among his friends at this school was Coleridge, with whom he formed a life-long friendship. In 1793, Lamb obtained an appointment in the India House, where he remained till 1825, when he was allowed to retire on a pension. Thus for all these long years Charles Lamb was a hard-worked clerk, and faithfully and patiently did he discharge the tedious duties of his position. In the year 1792, a terrible calamity befell his family. His sister Mary, a woman of the most estimable and amiable disposition, became suddenly insane, and in a frenzy grasped a knife and stabbed her mother to the heart. This event affected the whole life of Lamb. He gave up all thought of marriage, and thenceforth devoted his life to his beloved sister. She was ever afterward subject to fits of insanity; but when these attacks were over, she was a clever woman and a charming companion. "She was the only object between him and God," says Barry Cornwall, "and out of that misery and desolation sprung that wonderful love between brother and sister, which has no parallel in history." Mary, the "Bridget" of his essays, became his housekeeper. Their humble home was a favorite resort of many distinguished men of the time who have recorded their deep affection for the gifted brother and his gentle sister. Hard and dreary as was his daily life, Charles Lamb found time to read and re-read the great English prose-writers and dramatists, particularly of the sixteenth and seventeenth centuries. He so saturated his mind with much reading of these old authors, that his style has a peculiar and subtle charm. A certain quaintness and antiquity became the natural garb of his thoughts. Lamb is best known by his *Essays of Elia,* writings full of quaint humor and tender pathos. These essays, signed " Elia," were contributed to various London periodicals, between the years 1820 and 1833. Some of them, generally visions and parables, are incomparably simple and beautiful, as *The Child-Angel* and *Dream-Children*. Read also *New-Year's Eve, My First Play, Dissertation upon Roast Pig, Old China* and *Barbara S.*," as illustrations of these quaint, humorous and original essays. In conjunction with his sister, Lamb compiled several popular books for children. Among these is the *Tales from Shakespeare*, published in 1807, and consisting of twenty "tales" founded upon as many different plays of Shakespeare. Fourteen were written by Mary, and the remaining six, the great tragedies, by Charles. Of the tales in this number of the "English Classics," Mary wrote *The Tempest* and *The Merchant of Venice;* and Charles wrote *King Lear.* The success of the *Tales* was decisive and immediate. It has kept its place as a classic all these years, and serves to-day as a most popular and useful introduction to the study of Shakespeare. In a private letter to a friend, Mary Lamb wrote: "You would like to see us, as we often sit writing at one table, like Hermia and Helena in the *Midsummer Night's Dream;* or rather like an old literary Darby and Joan, I taking snuff and he groaning all the while and saying he can make nothing of it, which he always says till he has finished, and then he finds out he has made something of it."

A slight accident brought on erysipelas and "the gentle Elia" sinking rapidly, died in December, 1834. Mary survived her brother thirteen years and was laid in the same grave with him in May, 1847.

NOTE.—For collateral reading, consult Barry Cornwall's "Memoir of Charles Lamb," Ainger's Life and Anne Gilchrist's "Mary Lamb."

Extract from the Original Preface.

The following tales are meant to be submitted to the young reader as an introduction to the study of Shakespeare, for which purpose his words are used whenever it seemed possible to bring them in ; and in whatever has been added to them to give them the regular form of a connected story, diligent care has been taken to select such words as might least interrupt the effect of the beautiful English tongue in which he wrote. It is my wish that the true plays of Shakespeare may prove to you in older years, enrichers of the fancy, strengtheners of virtue, a withdrawing from all selfish and mercenary thought, a lesson of sweet and honorable thought and actions, to teach you courtesy, benignity, generosity, humanity; for of examples, teaching these virtues, his pages are full.—*Mary Lamb.*

LAMB'S
TALES FROM SHAKESPEARE.

THE TEMPEST.

" *The Tempest* is one of the most original and perfect of Shakespeare's productions, and he has shown in it all the variety of his powers. It is full of grace and grandeur. The humor and imaginary characters, the dramatic and the grotesque, are blended together with the greatest art, and without any appearance of it."
— *William Hazlitt.*

PREFATORY NOTE.

It is highly probable that this beautiful play was written in the year 1610 or 1611, when Shakespeare was about forty-seven years of age. The great dramatist usually founded his plays upon some well-known historical tale or romance. The story of *The Tempest* was probably borrowed from some old Italian or Spanish novel. Several points of resemblance render it probable that Shakespeare in writing the play had before him an account of a shipwreck in the Bermudas, written by Sylvester Jourdan. The fleet of Sir George Somers was wrecked on one of these islands in 1609, and the admiral's ship was driven ashore. Shakespeare makes mention in the first Act of "the still-vexed Bermoothes." Gonzalo's description of an imaginary commonwealth is borrowed from Florio's translation of Montaigne's Essays. A German dramatist named Ayrer, who died in 1605, was the author of a play, the plot of which has so much in common with the plot of *The Tempest* that it has been supposed that they must have had the same original.

"As to the actual scene of *The Tempest*," says Richard Grant White, " that is in the realms of fancy. Mr. Hunter has contended that Lampedusa, an island in the Mediterranean, lying not far out of a ship's course, passing from Tunis to Naples, and which is uninhabited, and supposed by sailors to be enchanted, was Prospero's place of exile. It may have been; though, if it were, we would a little rather not believe so. When the great magician at whose beck it rose from the waters broke his staff, the island sunk and carried Caliban down with it."

THERE was a certain island [1] in the sea, the only inhabitants of which were an old man, whose name was Prospero, and his daughter Miranda, a very beautiful young lady. She came to this island so young that she had no memory of having seen any other human face than her father's.

They lived in a cave or cell made out of a rock; it was divided into several apartments, one of which Prospero called his study; there he kept his books, which chiefly treated of magic, a study at that time much affected by all learned men; and the knowledge of this art he found very useful to him, for being thrown by a strange chance upon this island, which had been enchanted by a witch [2] called Sycorax, who died there a short time before his arrival, Prospero, by virtue of his art, released many good spirits that Sycorax had imprisoned in the bodies of large trees because they had refused to execute her wicked commands. These gentle spirits were ever after obedient to the will of Prospero. Of these Ariel was the chief.

The lively little sprite Ariel had nothing mischievous in his nature, except that he took rather too much pleasure in tormenting an ugly monster [3] called Caliban, for he owed him a grudge because he was the son of his old enemy Sycorax. This Caliban,

---

[1] **Certain island.**—There is good reason to believe that the early accounts of the Bermudas, then very lately made known to the English public, suggested to Shakespeare the general idea of his enchanted island, and gave it much of its picturesque and supernatural character.

[2] **Enchanted by a witch.**—It was the current opinion in Shakespeare's time, that the Bermudas and other far-away islands of the Western seas were inhabited by witches and monsters. They were associated, in the imagination of the people of that day, with vague ideas of terror and superstition.

[3] **Ugly monster.**—
                        "This misshapen knave,
His mother was a witch; and so strong
That could control the moon, make flow and ebbs,
And deal in her command without her power."

"Caliban has become a by-word, as the strange creation of a poetical imagination: a mixture of the gnome and the savage; half demon, half brute."—*Schlegel.*

Prospero found in the woods, a strange misshapen thing, far less human in form than an ape; he took him home to his cell and taught him to speak; and Prospero would have been very kind to him, but the bad nature which Caliban inherited from his mother Sycorax would not let him learn anything good or useful; therefore he was employed like a slave to fetch wood and do the most laborious offices, and Ariel had the charge of compelling him to these services.

When Caliban was lazy and neglected his work, Ariel (who was invisible to all eyes but Prospero's) would come slyly and pinch him, and sometimes tumble him down in the mire; and then Ariel, in the likeness of an ape, would make mouths at him; then swiftly changing his shape, in the likeness of a hedgehog he would lie tumbling in Caliban's way, who feared the hedgehog's sharp quills would prick his bare feet. With a variety of such-like vexatious tricks Ariel would often torment him whenever Caliban neglected the work which Prospero commanded him to do.

Having these powerful spirits obedient to his will, Prospero could by their means command the winds and the waves of the sea. By his orders they raised a violent storm, in the midst of which, and struggling with the wild sea-waves that every moment threatened to swallow it up, he showed his daughter a fine large ship, which he told her was full of living beings like themselves. "O my dear father," said she, "if by your art you have raised this dreadful storm, have pity on their sad distress. See! the vessel will be dashed to pieces. Poor souls! they will all perish. If I had the power I would sink the sea beneath the earth rather than the good ship should be destroyed, with all the precious souls within her."

"Be not so amazed, daughter Miranda," said Prospero; "there is no harm done. I have so ordered it, that no person in the ship shall receive any hurt. What I have done has been in care of you, my dear child. You are ignorant who you are, or where you came from, and you know no more of me but that I am your father and live in this poor cave. Can you remember a time before you came to this cell? I think you can not, for you were not then three years of age."

"Certainly I can, sir," replied Miranda.

"By what?" asked Prospero; "by any other house or person? Tell me what you can remember, my child."

Miranda said, "It seems to me like the recollection of a dream. But had I not once four or five women who attended upon me?"

Prospero answered, "You had, and more. How is it that this still lives in your mind? Do you remember how you came here?"

"No, sir," said Miranda. "I remember nothing more."

"Twelve years ago, Miranda," continued Prospero, "I was Duke of Milan, and you were a princess and my only heir. I had a younger brother, whose name was Antonio, to whom I trusted everything; and as I was fond of retirement and deep study, I commonly left the management of my state affairs to your uncle, my false brother (for so indeed he proved). I, neglecting all worldly ends, buried among my books, did dedicate my whole time to the bettering of my mind. My brother Antonio being thus in possession of my power began to think himself the Duke indeed. The opportunity I gave him of making himself popular among my subjects awakened in his bad nature a proud ambition to deprive me of my dukedom; this he soon effected with the aid of the King of Naples, a powerful prince, who was my enemy."

"Wherefore," said Miranda, "did they not that hour destroy us?"

"My child," answered her father, "they durst not, so dear was the love that my people bore me. Antonio carried us on board a ship, and when we were some leagues out at sea he forced us into a small boat without either tackle, sail, or mast; there he left us, as he thought, to perish. But a kind lord of my court, one Gonzalo, who loved me, had privately placed in the boat water, provisions, apparel, and some books, which I prize above my dukedom."

"O my father," said Miranda, "what a trouble I must have been to you then!"

" No, my love," said Prospero, " you were a little cherub that did preserve me. Your innocent smiles made me to bear up against my misfortunes. Our food lasted till we landed on this desert island, since when my chief delight has been in teaching you, Miranda, and well have you profited by my instructions."

"Heaven thank you, my dear father," said Miranda. "Now, pray tell me, sir, your reason for raising this sea-storm."

"Know then," said her father, "that by means of this storm my enemies, the King of Naples and my cruel brother, are cast ashore upon this island."

Having so said, Prospero gently touched his daughter with his magic wand and she fell fast asleep, for the spirit Ariel just then presented himself before his master to give an account of the tempest, and how he had disposed of the ship's company ; and though the spirits were always invisible to Miranda, Prospero did not choose she should hear him holding converse (as would seem to her) with the empty air.

"Well, my brave spirit," said Prospero to Ariel, "how have you performed your task ?"

Ariel gave a lively description of the storm, and of the terrors of the mariners; and how the king's son, Ferdinand, was the first who leaped into the sea ; and his father thought he saw this dear son swallowed up by the waves and lost. "But he is safe," said Ariel, "in a corner of the isle sitting with his arms folded, sadly lamenting the loss of the king, his father, whom he concludes drowned. Not a hair of his head is injured; and his princely garments, though drenched in the sea-waves, look fresher than before."

"That's my delicate Ariel," said Prospero. "Bring him hither: my daughter must see this young prince. Where is the king and my brother ?"

"I left them," answered Ariel, "searching for Ferdinand, whom they have little hopes of finding, thinking they saw him perish. Of the ship's crew, not one is missing, though each one thinks himself the only one saved ; and the ship, though invisible to them, is safe in the harbor."

"Ariel," said Prospero, "thy charge is faithfully performed; but there is more work yet."

"Is there more work?" said Ariel. "Let me remind you, master, you have promised me my liberty. I pray, remember I have done you worthy service, told you no lies, made no mistakes, served you without grudge or grumbling."

"How now?" said Prospero. "You do not recollect what a torment I freed you from. Have you forgot the wicked witch Sycorax, who, with age and envy, was almost bent double? Where was she born? Speak: tell me."

"Sir, in Algiers," said Ariel.

"Oh, was she so?" said Prospero. "I must recount what you have been, which I find you do not remember. This bad witch Sycorax, for her witchcrafts, too terrible to enter human hearing, was banished from Algiers and here left by the sailors; and because you were a spirit too delicate to execute her wicked commands she shut you up in a tree, where I found you howling. This torment, remember, I did free you from."

"Pardon me, dear master," said Ariel, ashamed to seem ungrateful; "I will obey your commands."

"Do so," said Prospero, "and I will set you free." He then gave orders what further he would have him do; and away went Ariel, first to where he had left Ferdinand, and found him still sitting on the grass in the same melancholy posture.

"Oh, my young gentleman," said Ariel, when he saw him, "I will soon move you. You must be brought, I find, for the Lady Miranda to have a sight of your pretty person. Come, sir, follow me." He then began singing—

> "Full fathom five thy father lies;
> Of his bones are coral made;
> Those are pearls that were his eyes
> Nothing of him that doth fade,
> But doth suffer a sea change
> Into something rich and strange.
> Sea-nymphs hourly ring his knell:
> Hark! now I hear them, ding-dong-bell."

This strange news of his lost father soon roused the prince

from the stupid fit into which he had fallen. He followed in amazement the sound of Ariel's voice till it led him to Prospero and Miranda, who were sitting under the shade of a large tree. Now Miranda had never seen a man before, except her own father.

"Miranda," said Prospero, "tell me what you are looking at yonder."

"O father," said Miranda, in a strange surprise, "surely that is a spirit. Lord! how it looks about! Believe me, sir, it is a beautiful creature. Is it not a spirit?"

"No, girl," answered her father; "it eats, and sleeps, and has senses such as we have. This young man you see was in the ship; he is somewhat altered by grief or you might call him a handsome person; he has lost his companions, and is wandering about to find them."

Miranda, who thought all men had grave faces and gray beards like her father, was delighted with the appearance of this beautiful young prince; and Ferdinand, seeing such a lovely lady in this desert place, and, from the strange sounds he heard, expecting nothing but wonders, thought he was upon an enchanted island, and that Miranda was the goddess of the place, and as such he began to address her.[1]

She timidly answered she was no goddess, but a simple maid, and was going to give him an account of herself, when Prospero interrupted her. He was well pleased to find they admired each other, for he plainly perceived they had (as we say) fallen in love at first sight; but to try Ferdinand's constancy, he resolved to throw some difficulties in their way; therefore, advancing forward, he addressed the prince with a stern air, telling him he came to the island as a spy, to take it from him who was the

---

[1] **Began to address her.**—Read this passage from the text:—
" Most sure, the goddess
On whom these airs attend! Vouchsafe my prayer
May know if you remain upon this island;
And that you some good instruction give
How I may bear me here: my prime request,
Which I do last pronounce, is, O you wonder
If you be maid or no?" etc.

lord of it. "Follow me," said he, "I will tie you neck and feet together. You shall drink sea-water; shell-fish, withered roots, and husks of acorns, shall be your food." "No," said Ferdinand, "I will resist such entertainment, till I see a more powerful enemy," and drew his sword; but Prospero, waving his magic wand, fixed him to the spot where he stood, so that he had no power to move.

Miranda hung upon her father, saying, "Why are you so ungentle? Have pity, sir; I will be his surety. This is the second man I ever saw, and to me he seems a true one."

"Silence," said her father, "one word more will make me chide you, girl! What! an advocate for an impostor! You think there are no more such fine men, having seen only him and Caliban. I tell you, foolish girl, most men as far excel this as he does Caliban." This he said to prove his daughter's constancy; and she replied, "My affections are most humble. I have no wish to see a goodlier man."

"Come on, young man," said Prospero to the prince, "you have no power to disobey me."

"I have not indeed," answered Ferdinand; and not knowing that it was by magic he was deprived of all power of resistance, he was astonished to find himself so strangely compelled to follow Prospero. Looking back on Miranda as long as he could see her, he said, as he went after Prospero into the cave, "My spirits are all bound up, as if I were in a dream; but this man's threats, and the weakness which I feel, would seem light to me if from my prison I might once a day behold this fair maid."

Prospero kept Ferdinand not long confined within the cell; he soon brought out his prisoner, and set him a severe task to perform, taking care to let his daughter know the hard labor he had imposed on him; and then pretending to go into his study, he secretly watched them both.

Prospero had commanded Ferdinand to pile up some heavy logs of wood. King's sons not being much used to laborious work, Miranda soon after found her lover[1] almost dying with

---

[1] **Miranda . . . . found her lover.**—This interview between Miranda and Ferdinand, described in the First Scene of Act Third, is one of the most charming passages to be found in Shakespeare.

fatigue. "Alas!" said she, "do not work so hard; my father is at his studies, he is safe for these three hours; pray rest yourself."

"O my dear lady," said Ferdinand, "I dare not. I must finish my task before I take my rest."

"If you will sit down," said Miranda, "I will carry your logs the while." But this Ferdinand would by no means agree to. Instead of a help, Miranda became a hindrance, for they began a long conversation, so that the business of log-carrying went on very slowly.

Prospero, who had enjoined Ferdinand this task merely as a trial of his love, was not at his books as his daughter supposed, but was standing by them invisible, to overhear what they said.

Ferdinand inquired her name, which she told him, saying it was against her father's express command she did so.

Prospero only smiled at this first instance of his daughter's disobedience, for having by his magic art caused his daughter to fall in love so suddenly, he was not angry that she showed her love by forgetting to obey his commands. And he listened well pleased to a long speech of Ferdinand's, in which he professed to love her above all the ladies he ever saw.

In answer to his praises of her beauty,[1] which he said exceeded all the women in the world, she replied, "I do not remember the face of any woman, nor have I seen any more men than you, my good friend, and my dear father. How features are abroad, I know not; but believe me, sir, I would not wish any companion in the world but you, nor can my imagination form any shape but yours that I could like. But, sir, I fear I talk to you too freely, and my father's precepts I forget."

At this Prospero smiled, and nodded his head, as much as to say. "This goes on exactly as I could wish; my girl will be Queen of Naples."

And then Ferdinand, in another fine long speech (for young princes speak in courtly phrases), told the innocent Miranda he was heir to the crown of Naples, and that she should be his queen.

---

[1] **Praises of her beauty.**—Read this passage in Act III., Scene 1:—
"Admired Miranda!
Indeed the top of admiration; worth
What's dearest to the world!" etc.

"Ah, sir," said she, "I am a fool to weep at what I am glad of. I will answer you in plain and holy innocence. I am your wife, if you will marry me."

Prospero prevented Ferdinand's thanks by appearing visible before them.

"Fear nothing, my child," said he; "I have overheard and approve of all you have said. And, Ferdinand, if I have too severely used you, I will make you rich amends by giving you my daughter. All your vexations were but my trials of your love, and you have nobly stood the test. Then as my gift, which your true love has worthily purchased, take my daughter, and do not smile that I boast she is above all praise." He then, telling them that he had business which required his presence, desired they would sit down and talk together till he returned; and this command Miranda seemed not at all disposed to disobey.

When Prospero left them, he called his spirit Ariel, who quickly appeared before him, eager to relate what he had done with Prospero's brother and the King of Naples. Ariel said he had left them almost out of their senses with fear, at the strange things he had caused them to see and hear. When fatigued with wandering about, and famished for want of food, he had suddenly set before them a delicious banquet, and then, just as they were going to eat, he appeared visible before them in the shape of a harpy, a voracious monster with wings, and the feast vanished away. Then, to their utter amazement, this seeming harpy spoke to them, reminding them of their cruelty in driving Prospero from his dukedom, and leaving him and his infant daughter to perish in the sea, saying, that for this cause these terrors were suffered to afflict them.

The King of Naples, and Antonio the false brother, repented the injustice [1] they had done to Prospero; and Ariel told his

---

[1] **Repented the injustice.**—Read the King's penitent words in Act III., Scene 3:—

> " O, it is monstrous, monstrous!
> Methought the billows spoke and told me of it
> The winds did sing it to me; and the thunder,
> That deep and dreadful organ-pipe, pronounc'd
> The name of Prosper," etc.

master he was certain their penitence was sincere, and that he, though a spirit, could not but pity them.

"Then bring them hither, Ariel," said Prospero; "if you, who are but a spirit, feel for their distress, shall not I, who am a human being like themselves, have compassion on them? Bring them quickly, my dainty Ariel."

Ariel soon returned with the King, Antonio, and old Gonzalo in their train, who had followed him, wondering at the wild music he played in the air to draw them on to his master's presence. This Gonzalo was the same who had so kindly provided Prospero formerly with books and provisions, when his wicked brother left him, as he thought, to perish in an open boat in the sea.

Grief and terror had so stupefied their senses, that they did not know Prospero. He first discovered himself to the good old Gonzalo, calling him the preserver of his life; and then his brother and the king knew that he was the injured Prospero.

Antonio, with tears and sad words of sorrow and true repentance, implored his brother's forgiveness, and the king expressed his sincere remorse for having assisted Antonio to depose his brother: and Prospero forgave them; and, upon their engaging to restore his dukedom, he said to the King of Naples, "I have a gift in store for you too;" and opening a door, showed him his son Ferdinand, playing at chess[1] with Miranda.

Nothing could exceed the joy of the father and the son at this unexpected meeting, for they each thought the other drowned in the storm.

"O wonder!" said Miranda, "what noble creatures these are! It must surely be a brave world that has such people in it."

The King of Naples was almost as much astonished at the beauty and excellent graces of the young Miranda, as his son had

---

[1] **Playing at chess.**—Read the delightful passage, (Act V., Scene 1), in which Prospero discovers Ferdinand and Miranda playing at chess.

"Miranda is a character blending the truth of nature with the most exquisite refinement of poetic fancy, unrivalled, even in Shakespeare's own long and beautiful series of portraitures of feminine excellence."—*G. C. Verplanck.*

been. "Who is this maid?" said he; "she seems the goddess that has parted us, and brought us thus together." "No, sir," answered Ferdinand, smiling to find that his father had fallen into the same mistake that he had done when he first saw Miranda, "she is a mortal, but by immortal Providence she is mine; I chose her when I could not ask you, my father, for your consent, not thinking you were alive. She is the daughter to this Prospero, who is the famous Duke of Milan, of whose renown I have heard so much, but never saw him till now: of him I have received a new life: he has made himself to me a second father, giving me this dear lady."

"Then I must be her father," said the king; "but oh! how oddly will it sound, that I must ask my child forgiveness."

"No more of that," said Prospero; "let us not remember our troubles past, since they so happily have ended." And then Prospero embraced his brother, and again assured him of his forgiveness; and said that a wise, over-ruling Providence had permitted that he should be driven from his poor dukedom of Milan, that his daughter might inherit the crown of Naples, for that by their meeting in this desert island, it happened that the king's son had loved Miranda.

These kind words which Prospero spoke, meaning to comfort his brother, so filled Antonio with shame and remorse, that he wept and was unable to speak; and the kind old Gonzalo wept to see this joyful reconciliation, and prayed for blessings on the young couple.

Prospero now told them that their ship was safe in the harbor, and the sailors all on board her, and that he and his daughter would accompany them home the next morning. "In the meantime," said he, "partake of such refreshments as my poor cave affords; and for your evening's entertainment [1] I will relate the history of my life from my first landing in this desert island."

---

[1] **Evening entertainment.**—Prospero gives his daughter and her lover an exhibition of his magic art.

> "For I must
> Bestow upon the eyes of this young couple
> Some vanity of mine art: it is my promise,
> And they expect it from me."

He then called for Caliban to prepare some food, and set the cave in order; and the company were astonished at the uncouth form and savage appearance of this ugly monster, who (Prospero said) was the only attendant he had to wait upon him.

Before Prospero left the island, he dismissed Ariel from his service, to the great joy of that lively little spirit; who, though he had been a faithful servant to his master, was always longing to enjoy his free liberty, to wander uncontrolled in the air, like a wild bird, under green trees, among pleasant fruits and sweet smiling flowers. "My quaint Ariel," said Prospero to the little sprite when he made him free, "I shall miss you; yet you shall have your freedom." "Thank you, my dear master," said Ariel; "but give me leave to attend your ship home with prosperous gales, before you bid farewell to the assistance of your faithful spirit; and then, master, when I am free, how merrily I shall live!" Here Ariel sung this pretty song—

"Where the bee sucks, there suck I;
In a cowslip's bell I lie:
There I couch when owls do cry.
On the bat's back do I fly
After summer merrily.
Merrily, merrily, shall I live now
Under the blossom that hangs on the bough."

Prospero then buried deep in the earth his magical books and wand,[1] for he was resolved never more to make use of the magic art. After having thus overcome his enemies, and being reconciled to his brother and the King of Naples, nothing now remained to complete his happiness, but to revisit his native land, to take possession of his dukedom, and to witness the happy

Revels follow, in which Iris, Ceres and Juno appear. Read and commit to memory the closing words with which Prospero dismisses the spirits:—
"Our revels now are ended. These our actors,
As I foretold you, were all spirits, and
Are melted into air, into thin air:" etc.—Act IV., Scene 1.

[1] **Buried deep . . . . his magical books and wand.**—
"This rough magic
I here abjure;—I'll break my staff,
Bury it certain fathoms in the earth,
And deeper than did ever plummet sound
I'll drown my book."

nuptials of his daughter Miranda and Prince Ferdinand, which the king said should be instantly celebrated with great splendor on their return to Naples. At which place, under the safe convoy of the spirit Ariel, they, after a pleasant voyage, soon arrived.

THE MERCHANT OF VENICE.

" The more we study the work, the more we cannot but wonder that- so much of human nature, in so great a variety of development, should be crowded into so small a space.—*H. N. Hudson.*

PREFATORY NOTE.

THERE is good reason to believe that *The Merchant of Venice,* one of Shakespeare's most perfect works, was written and acted as early as 1594. The plot of the play is made up of two distinct stories ; that of the bond, and that of the caskets, fables told separately many times and in many countries. Both stories are found in a collection of tales, popular in the Middle Ages, called *Gesta Romanorum,* translated into English during the reign of Henry VI. The immediate source from which Shakespeare derived the incident of the pound of flesh is probably a collection of tales written by an Italian author about 1378, but first published at Milan in 1558. It is not unlikely that the stories of the play may have been worked over by the genius of Shakespeare from old and useless dramatic material, found in the crude productions of the early English theatre. The question is not of any great importance. " Be the merit of the fable whose it may," says an eminent Shakespearean scholar, " the characters, the language, the poetry, and the sentiment are his, and his alone. To no other writer of the period could we be indebted for the charming combination of womanly grace and dignity and playfulness which is found in Portia ; for the exquisite picture of friendship between Bassanio and Antonio ; for the profusion of poetic beauties scattered over the play ; and for the masterly delineation of that perfect type of Judaism in olden times, the character of Shylock himself.

Shylock, the Jew, lived at Venice: he was an usurer, who had amassed an immense fortune by lending money at great interest to Christian merchants. Shylock being a hard-hearted man, exacted the payment of the money he lent, with such severity, that he was much disliked by all good men, and particularly by Antonio, a young merchant of Venice; and Shylock as much hated Antonio, because he used to lend money to people in distress, and would never take any interest for the money he lent; therefore there was great enmity between this covetous Jew and the generous merchant Antonio. Whenever Antonio met Shylock on the Rialto,[1] he used to reproach him with his usuries and hard-dealings; which the Jew would bear with seeming patience, while he secretly meditated revenge.

Antonio was the kindest man that lived, the best conditioned, and had the most unwearied spirit in doing courtesies; indeed, he was one in which the ancient Roman honor more appeared than in any that drew breath in Italy. He was greatly beloved by all his fellow-citizens; but the friend who was nearest and dearest to his heart was Bassanio, a noble Venetian, who, having but a small patrimony, had nearly exhausted his little fortune by living in too expensive a manner for his slender means, as young men of high rank with small fortunes are apt to do. Whenever Bassanio wanted money, Antonio assisted him; and it seemed as if they had but one heart and one purse between them.

One day Bassanio came to Antonio, and told him that he wished to repair his fortune by a wealthy marriage with a lady whom he dearly loved, whose father, that was lately dead, had left her sole heiress to a large estate; and that in her father's lifetime he used to visit at her house, when he thought he had observed this lady had sometimes from her eyes sent speechless messages, that seemed to say he would be no unwelcome suitor; but not having money to furnish himself with an appearance befitting the lover of so rich an heiress, he besought Antonio to add to the many favors he had shown him by lending him

---

[1] Rialto.—The chief of the islands on which Venice is built. The name Rialto came also to be applied to the Exchange which was on that island.

three thousand ducats. Antonio had no money by him at that time to lend his friend; but expecting soon to have some ships come home laden with merchandise, he said he would go to Shylock, the rich money-lender, and borrow the money upon the credit of those ships.

Antonio and Bassanio went together to Shylock, and Antonio asked the Jew to lend him three thousand ducats [1] upon any interest he should require, to be paid out of the merchandise contained in his ships at sea. On this Shylock thought within himself: "If I can once catch him on the hip, [2] I will feed fat the ancient grudge I bear him; he hates our Jewish nation; he lends out money gratis; and among the merchants he rails at me and my well-earned bargains, which he calls interest. Cursed be my tribe, if I forgive him!" Antonio, finding he was musing within himself and did not answer, and being impatient for the money, said, "Shylock, do you hear? will you lend the money?" To this question the Jew replied, "Signior Antonio, on the Rialto many a time and often you have railed at me about my moneys, and my usuries, and I have borne it with a patient shrug, for sufferance is the badge of all our tribe: and then you have called me an unbeliever, cut-throat dog, and spit upon my Jewish garments, and spurned at me with your foot, as if I was a cur. Well, then, it now appears you need my help; and you come to me and say, *Shylock, lend me moneys.* Has a dog money? Is it possible a cur should lend three thousand ducats? Shall I bend low and say, Fair sir, you spit upon me on Wednesday last, another time you called me dog, and for these courtesies I am to lend you moneys." Antonio replied, "I am as like to call you so again, to spit on you again, and spurn you too. If you will lend me this money, lend it not to me as to a friend, but rather lend it to me as to an enemy, that, if I break, you may with better face exact the penalty." "Why, look you," said Shylock, "how you storm! I would be friends with you, and have your

---

[1] **Three thousand ducats.**—The value of the Venetian ducat, in Shakespeare's day, was about $1.50.

[2] **On the hip.**—To have the advantage over one. A phrase used by wrestlers.

love. I will forget the shames you have put upon me. I will supply your wants, and take no interest for my money." This seemingly kind offer greatly surprised Antonio; and then Shylock, still pretending kindness, and that all he did was to gain Antonio's love, again said he would lend him the three thousand ducats, and take no interest for his money; only Antonio should go with him to a lawyer, and there sign in merry sport a bond, that if he did not repay the money by a certain day, he would forfeit a pound of flesh,[1] to be cut off from any part of his body that Shylock pleased.

"Content," said Antonio; "I will sign to this bond, and say there is much kindness in the Jew." Bassanio said Antonio should not sign to such a bond for him; but still Antonio insisted that he would sign it, for that before the day of payment came, his ships would return laden with many times the value of the money.

Shylock, hearing this debate, exclaimed, "O father Abraham, what suspicious people these Christians are! their own hard dealings teach them to suspect the thoughts of others. I pray you tell me this, Bassanio; if he should break this day, what should I gain by the exaction of the forfeiture? A pound of man's flesh taken from a man, is not so estimable, nor profitable neither, as the flesh of mutton or of beef. I say, to buy his favor I offer this friendship: if he will take it, so; if not, adieu."

At last, against the advice of Bassanio, who, notwithstanding all the Jew had said of his kind intentions, did not like his friend should run the hazard of this shocking penalty for his sake, Antonio signed the bond, thinking it really was (as the Jew said) merely in sport.

The rich heiress that Bassanio wished to marry lived near Venice, at a place called Belmont; her name was Portia, and in the graces of her person and her mind she was nothing inferior to that Portia, of whom we read, who was Cato's daughter, and

---

[1] **Pound of flesh.**—The story of the pound of flesh is one of the many traditionary narratives which has traveled round the world, reappearing in varied forms, in different ages, countries and languages.

the wife of Brutus. Bassanio, being so kindly supplied with money by his friend Antonio at the hazard of his life, set out for Belmont with a splendid train, and attended by a gentleman of the name of Gratiano. Bassanio proving successful in his suit,[1] Portia in a short time consented to accept of him for a husband.

Bassanio confessed to Portia that he had no fortune, and that his high birth and noble ancestry was all that he could boast of; she, who loved him for his worthy qualities, and had riches enough not to regard wealth in a husband, answered with a graceful modesty,[2] that she would wish herself a thousand times more fair, and ten thousand times more rich, to be more worthy of him; and then the accomplished Portia prettily dispraised herself, and said she was an unlessoned girl, unschooled, unpractised, yet not so old but that she could learn, and that she would commit her gentle spirit to be directed and governed by him in all things; and she said, "Myself and what is mine, to you and yours is now converted. But yesterday, Bassanio, I was the lady of this fair mansion, queen of myself, and mistress over these servants; and now this house, these servants, and myself, are yours, my lord; I give them with this ring:" presenting a ring to Bassanio. Bassanio was so overpowered with gratitude and wonder at the gracious manner in which the rich and noble Portia accepted of a man of his humble fortunes, that he could not express his joy and reverence to the dear lady who so honored him, by anything but broken words of love and thankfulness; and taking the ring, he vowed never to part with it.

Gratiano and Nerissa, Portia's waiting-maid, were in attendance upon their lord and lady, when Portia so gracefully promised to become the obedient wife of Bassanio; and Gratiano, wishing Bassanio and the generous lady joy, desired permission

---

[1] **Successful in his suit.**—All reference to the "casket scenes," in which the suitors of the fair Portia are doomed to disappointment, except Bassanio, is here omitted. See the text, Act II., and Act III., Scene 2.

[2] **Answered .... graceful modesty.**—Read and commit the passage, Act III., Scene 2 :—

"You see me, Lord Bassanio, where I stand,
Such as I am," etc.

to be married at the same time. " With all my heart, Gratiano," said Bassanio, " if you can get a wife."

Gratiano then said that he loved the lady Portia's fair waiting gentlewoman, Nerissa, and that she had promised to be his wife, if her lady married Bassanio. Portia asked Nerissa if this was true. Nerissa replied, " Madam, it is so, if you approve of it." Portia willingly consenting, Bassanio pleasantly said, " Then our wedding-feast shall be much honored by your marriage, Gratiano."

The happiness of these lovers was sadly crossed at this moment by the entrance of a messenger, who brought a letter from Antonio containing fearful tidings. When Bassanio read Antonio's letter, Portia feared that it was to tell him of the death of some dear friend, he looked so pale; and inquiring what was the news which had so distressed him, he said, " O sweet Portia, here are a few of the unpleasantest words that ever blotted paper: gentle lady, when I first imparted my love to you, I freely told you all the wealth I had ran in my veins; but I should have told you I had less than nothing, being in debt." Bassanio then told Portia what has been here related, of his borrowing the money of Antonio, and of Antonio's procuring it of Shylock the Jew, and of the bond by which Antonio had engaged to forfeit a pound of flesh, if it was not repaid by a certain day; and then Bassanio read Antonio's letter, the words of which were: " *Sweet Bassanio, my ships are all lost, my bond to the Jew is forfeited; and since in paying it, it is impossible I should live, I could wish to see you at my death. Notwithstanding, use your pleasure; if your love for me do not persuade you to come, let not my letter.*" " Oh my dear love," said Portia, " despatch all business and begone; you shall have gold to pay his money twenty times over, before this kind friend shall lose a hair by my Bassanio's fault; and as you are so dearly bought, I will dearly love you." Portia then said she would be married to Bassanio before he set out, to give him a legal right to the money; and that same day they were married, and Gratiano was also married to Nerissa; and Bassanio and Gratiano, the instant they were married, set out in great haste for Venice, where Bassanio found Antonio in prison. The day of paying being past, the cruel Jew would not accept of the money which Bassanio offered him, but insisted upon having a pound of Antonio's flesh. A day was appointed to try this shocking cause before the Duke of Venice, and Bassanio awaited in dreadful suspense the event of the trial.

When Portia parted with her husband, she spoke cheeringly to him, and bade. him bring his dear friend along with him when he returned; yet she feared it would go hard with Antonio, and when she was left alone, she began to think and consider within herself, if she could by any means be instrumental in saving the life of her dear Bassanio's friend; and notwithstanding, when she wished to honor her Bassanio, she had said to him with such a meek, wife-like grace, that she would submit in all things to be governed by his superior wisdom, yet being now called forth into action by the peril of her honored husband's friend, she did nothing doubt her own powers, and by the sole guidance of her own true and perfect judgment, at once resolved to go herself to Venice, and speak in Antonio's defence. Portia had a relation who was a counsellor in the law; to this gentleman, whose name was Bellario, she wrote, and stating the case to him, desired his opinion, and that with his advice he would also send the dress worn by a counsellor. When the messenger returned, he brought letters from Bellario of advice how to proceed, and also everything necessary for her equipment.

Portia dressed herself and her maid Nerissa in men's apparel, and putting on the robes of a counsellor,[1] she took Nerissa along with her as her clerk; and setting out immediately, they arrived at Venice on the very day of the trial. The cause was just going to be heard before the duke and senators of Venice in the senate-house, when Portia entered this high court of justice, and pre-

---

[1] **Robes of a counsellor.**—An old writer describes the dress of a doctor of laws, the habit in which Portia defends Antonio. The upper robe was of black damask cloth, velvet, or silk, according to the weather. The under one black silk, with a silk sash, the ends of which hang down to the middle of the leg; the stockings of black cloth or velvet; the cap of rich velvet or silk.

sented a letter from Bellario, in which that learned counsellor wrote to the duke, saying he would have come himself to plead for Antonio, but he was prevented by sickness, and he requested that the learned young doctor Balthasar (so he called Portia) might be permitted to plead in his stead. This the duke granted, much wondering at the youthful appearance of the stranger, who was prettily disguised by her counsellor's robes and her large wig.

And now began this important trial.[1] Portia looked around her, and she saw the merciless Jew; and she saw Bassanio, but he knew her not in her disguise. He was standing beside Antonio, in an agony of distress and fear for his friend.

The importance of the arduous task Portia had engaged in, gave this tender lady courage, and she boldly proceeded in the duty she had undertaken to perform; and first of all she addressed herself to Shylock; and allowing that he had a right by the Venetian law to have the forfeit expressed in the bond, she spoke so sweetly of the noble quality of *mercy*,[2] as would have softened any heart but the unfeeling Shylock's; saying, that it dropped as the gentle rain from heaven upon the place beneath; and how mercy was a double blessing, it blessed him that gave, and him that received it; and how it became monarchs better than their crowns, being an attribute of God himself; and that earthly power came nearest to God's in proportion as mercy tempered justice; and she bid Shylock remember that as we all pray for mercy, that same prayer should teach us to show mercy.

---

[1] **This important trial.**—Read and study this great trial scene, which is in Act IV. of the play. The incidents in this beautiful play are certainly not of every-day occurrence, yet they are such as might have actually occurred in the times and countries in which Shakespeare has placed his drama. It will be remembered that Shakespeare lived in the height of the legal controversy between the strict and literal old common-law and the equitable doctrine, on the subject of bonds and penalty. The old common-law held, that on the forfeiture of the bond, or a default of payment, the whole penalty was recoverable. It was highly probable that there were many well-known instances of hardship in enforcing penalties familiar to London citizens at the time *The Merchant of Venice* was written.

[2] **Quality of mercy.**—Read and commit to memory the exact words of the famous plea by Portia; nineteen lines, Act IV., Scene 1, beginning :—

" The quality of mercy is not strained,
It droppeth as the gentle rain from heaven
Upon the place beneath," etc.

Shylock only answered her by desiring to have the penalty forfeited in the bond. "Is he not able to pay the money?" asked Portia. Bassanio then offered the Jew the payment of the three thousand ducats as many times over as he should desire; which Shylock refusing and still insisting upon having a pound of Antonio's flesh, Bassanio begged the learned young counsellor would endeavor to wrest the law a little to save Antonio's life. But Portia gravely answered, that laws once established must never be altered. Shylock hearing Portia say that the law might not be altered, it seemed to him that she was pleading in his favor, and he said, "A Daniel is come to judgment! O wise young judge, how I do honor you! How much older are you than your looks!"

Portia now desired Shylock to let her look at the bond; and when she had read it, she said, "This bond is forfeited, and by this the Jew may lawfully claim a pound of flesh, to be by him cut off nearest Antonio's heart." Then she said to Shylock, "Be merciful; take the money, and bid me tear the bond." But no mercy would the cruel Shylock show; and he said, "By my soul I swear, there is no power in the tongue of man to alter me." "Why, then, Antonio," said Portia, "you must prepare your bosom for the knife;" and while Shylock was sharpening a long knife with great eagerness to cut off the pound of flesh, Portia said to Antonio, "Have you anything to say?" Antonio, with calm resignation, replied, that he had but little to say, for that he had prepared his mind for death. Then he said to Bassanio, "Give me your hand, Bassanio! Fare you well! Grieve not that I am fallen into this misfortune for you. Commend me to your honorable wife, and tell her how I have loved you!" Bassanio in the deepest affliction replied, "Antonio, I am married to a wife who is as dear to me as life itself; but life itself, my wife, and all the world, are not esteemed with me above your life. I would lose all, I would sacrifice all to this devil here, to deliver you."

Portia hearing this, though the kind-hearted lady was not at all offended with her husband for expressing the love he owed to so true a friend as Antonio in those strong terms, yet could not help answering, "Your wife would give you little thanks, if she were present, to hear you make this offer." And then Gratiano, who loved to copy what his lord did, thought he must make a speech like Bassanio's, and he said, in Nerissa's hearing, who was writing in her clerk's dress by the side of Portia, "I have a wife, whom I protest I love; I wish she were in heaven, if she could but entreat some power there to change the cruel temper of this currish Jew." "It is well you wish this behind her back, else you would have but an unquiet house," said Nerissa. Shylock now cried out, impatiently, "We trifle time; I pray pronounce the sentence." And now all was awful expectation in the court, and every heart was full of grief for Antonio.

Portia asked if the scales were ready to weigh the flesh; and she said to the Jew, "Shylock, you must have some surgeon by, lest he bleed to death." Shylock, whose whole intent was that Antonio should bleed to death, said, "It is not so named in the bond." Portia replied, "It is not so named in the bond, but what of that? It is good you did so much for charity." To this, all the answer that Shylock would make was, "I cannot find it; it is not in the bond." "Then," said Portia, "a pound of Antonio's flesh is thine. The law allows it, and the court awards it. And you may cut this flesh from off his breast. The law allows it, and the court awards it." Again Shylock exclaimed, "O wise and upright judge! A Daniel is come to judgment!" And then he sharpened his long knife again, and looking eagerly on Antonio, he said, "Come, prepare!"

"Tarry a little, Jew," said Portia; "there is something else. This bond here gives you no drop of blood; the words expressly are, a pound of flesh. If in the cutting off the pound of flesh you shed one drop of Christian blood, your land and goods are by the law to be confiscated to the state of Venice." Now, as it was utterly impossible for Shylock to cut off the pound of flesh without shedding some of Antonio's blood, this wise discovery of Portia's, that it was flesh and not blood that was named in the bond, saved the life of Antonio; and all admiring the wonderful sagacity of the young counsellor, who had so happily thought of this expedient, plaudits resounded from every part of the senate-house; and Gratiano exclaimed, in the words which Shylock had used, "O wise and upright judge! mark, Jew, a Daniel is come to judgment!"

Shylock finding himself defeated in his cruel intent, said, with a disappointed look, that he would take the money; and Bassanio, rejoiced beyond measure at Antonio's unexpected deliverance, cried out, "Here is the money!" But Portia stopped him, saying, "Softly; there is no haste; the Jew shall have nothing but the penalty; therefore prepare, Shylock, to cut off the flesh; but mind you shed no blood; nor do not cut off more nor less than just a pound: be it more or less by one poor scruple, nay, if the scale turn but by the weight of a single hair, you are condemned by the laws of Venice to die, and all your wealth is forfeited to the senate." "Give me my money, and let me go," said Shylock. "I have it ready," said Bassanio; "here it is."

Shylock was going to take the money, when Portia again stopped him saying, "Tarry, Jew; I have yet another hold upon you. By the laws of Venice, your wealth is forfeited to the state, for having conspired against the life of one of its citizens, and your life lies at the mercy of the duke; therefore down on your knees, and ask him to pardon you." The duke then said to Shylock, "That you may see the difference of our Christian spirit, I pardon you your life before you ask it; half your wealth belongs to Antonio, the other half comes to the state." The generous Antonio then said, that he would give up his share of Shylock's wealth, if Shylock would sign a deed to make it over at his death to his daughter and her husband: for Antonio knew that the Jew had an only daughter, who had lately married against his consent to a young Christian named Lorenzo, a friend of Antonio's, which had so offended Shylock, that he had disinherited her. The Jew agreed to this; and, being thus disappointed in his revenge, and despoiled of his riches, he said, "I am ill. Let me go home; send the deed after me, and I will sign over half my riches to my daughter." "Get thee gone then," said the duke, "and sign it; and if you repent your cruelty and turn Christian, the state will forgive you the fine of the other half of your riches."

The duke now released Antonio, and dismissed the court. He then highly praised the wisdom and ingenuity of the young counsellor, and invited him home to dinner. Portia, who meant to return to Belmont before her husband, replied, "I humbly thank your grace, but I must away directly." The duke said he was sorry he had not leisure to stay and dine with him; and, turning to Antonio, he added, " Reward this gentleman; for in my mind you are much indebted to him."

The duke and his senators left the court; and then Bassanio said to Portia, " Most worthy gentleman, I and my friend, Antonio, have, by your wisdom, been this day acquitted of grievous penalties, and I beg you will accept of the three thousand ducats due unto the Jew."

" And we shall stand indebted to you over and above," said Antonio, " in love and service evermore."

Portia could not be prevailed upon to accept the money; but upon Bassanio still pressing her to accept of some reward, she said, " Give me your gloves; I will wear them for your sake; " and then Bassanio taking off his gloves, she espied the ring which she had given him upon his finger. Now it was the ring the wily lady wanted to get from him to make a merry jest when she saw her Bassanio again, that made her ask him for his gloves; and she said, when she saw the ring, " And for your love I will take this ring from you." Bassanio was sadly distressed, that the counsellor should ask him for the only thing he could not part with, and he replied in great confusion, that he could not give him that ring, because it was his wife's gift, and he had vowed never to part with it; but that he would give him the most valuable ring in Venice, and find it out by proclamation. On this Portia affected to be affronted, and left the court, saying, " You teach me, sir, how a beggar should be answered." " Dear Bassanio," said Antonio, " let him have the ring; let my love and the great service he has done for me be valued against your wife's displeasure." Bassanio, ashamed to appear so ungrateful, yielded, and sent Gratiano after Portia with the ring; and then the clerk Nerissa, who had also given Gratiano a ring, she begged his ring, and Gratiano (not choosing to be outdone in generosity by his lord) gave it to her. And there was laughing among those ladies to think, when they got home, how they would tax their husbands with giving away their rings, and swear that they had given them as a present to some woman.

Portia, when she returned, was in that happy temper of mind

which never fails to attend the consciousness of having performed a good action; her cheerful spirits enjoyed everything she saw; the moon never seemed to shine so bright before;[1] and when that pleasant moon was hid behind a cloud, then a light which she saw from her house at Belmont as well pleased her charmed fancy, and she said to Nerissa, "That light we see is burning in my hall; how far that little candle throws its beams, so shines a good deed in a naughty world; and hearing the sound of music from her house, she said, "Methinks that music sounds much sweeter than by day." And now Portia and Nerissa entered the house, and dressing themselves in their own apparel, they awaited the arrival of their husbands, who soon followed them with Antonio; and Bassanio presenting his dear friend to the lady Portia, the congratulations and welcomings of that lady were hardly over, when they perceived Nerissa and her husband quarrelling in a corner of the room. "A quarrel already!" said Portia. "What is the matter?" Gratiano replied, "Lady, it is about a paltry gilt ring that Nerissa gave me, with words upon it like the poetry on a cutler's knife, '*Love me, and leave me not.*'"

"What does the poetry or the value of the ring signify?" said Nerissa. "You swore to me, when I gave it to you, that you would keep it till the hour of death; and now you say you gave it to the lawyer's clerk. I know you gave it to a woman." "By this hand," replied Gratiano, "I gave it to a youth, a kind of boy, a little scrubbed boy no higher than yourself; he was clerk to the young counsellor, that by his wise pleading saved Antonio's life; this prating boy begged it for a fee, and I could not for my life deny him." Portia said, "You were to blame, Gratiano, to part with your wife's first gift. I gave my lord Bassanio a ring, and I am sure he would not part with it for all the world." Gratiano in excuse for his fault now said, "My lord Bassanio gave his ring away to the counsellor, and then the boy, his clerk, that took some pains in writing, he begged my ring."

Portia, hearing this, seemed very angry, and reproached Bas-

---

[1] **Moon . . . . so bright before.**—Read and study the first part of Act V., until the beauty and truth of this exquisite night scene is fully realized. Commit the twelve lines beginning :—
" How sweet the moonlight sleeps upon this bank !" etc.

sanio for giving away her ring; and she said, Nerissa had taught her what to believe, and that she knew some woman had the ring. Bassanio was very unhappy to have so offended his dear lady, and he said with great earnestness, "No, by my honor, no woman had it, but a civil doctor, who refused three thousand ducats of me, and begged the ring, which when I denied him he went displeased away. What could I do, sweet Portia? I was so beset with shame for my seeming ingratitude, that I was forced to send the ring after him. Pardon me, good lady; had you been there, I think you would have begged the ring of me to give the worthy doctor."

"Ah!" said Antonio, "I am the unhappy cause of these quarrels."

Portia bade Antonio not to grieve at that, for that he was welcome notwithstanding; and then Antonio said, "I once did lend my body for Bassanio's sake, and but for him to whom your husband gave the ring, I should have now been dead. I dare be bound again, my soul upon the forfeit, your lord will never more break his faith with you."

"Then you shall be his surety," said Portia; "give him this ring, and bid him keep it better than the other."

When Bassanio looked at this ring, he was strangely surprised to find it was the same he gave away; and then Portia told him, how she was the young counsellor, and Nerissa was her clerk; and Bassanio found to his unspeakable wonder and delight, that it was by the noble courage and wisdom of his wife that Antonio's life was saved.

And Portia again welcomed Antonio, and gave him letters which by some chance had fallen into her hands, which contained an account of Antonio's ships that were supposed lost, being safely arrived in the harbor. So these tragical beginnings of this rich merchant's story were all forgotten in the unexpected good fortune which ensued, and there was leisure to laugh at the comical adventure of the rings, and the husbands that did not know their own wives: Gratiano merrily declaring, in a sort of rhyming speech, that—

> ——while he liv'd, he'd fear no other thing
> So sore, as keeping safe Nerissa's ring.

KING LEAR.

"The tragedy of *Lear* is deservedly celebrated among the dramas of Shakespeare. There is, perhaps, no play which keeps the attention so strongly fixed; which so much agitates our passions, and interests our curiosity."—*Dr. Johnson.*

PREFATORY NOTE.

IT is highly probable that the great tragedy of King Lear was written between 1603 and the end of 1606. It was first acted before James I. on the 26th of December, 1606, at Whitehall. The story of King Lear and his three daughters is one of the oldest stories in literature, and is found in many countries. It is told by Geoffrey of Monmouth, in his *Historia Britonum,* and was probably derived by him from some Welsh legendary source. The legend is told by Layamon in his *Brut ;* by Hollinshed in his *Chronicle ;* by Spenser in his *Faerie Quéene,* and by a ballad-writer whose poem is printed in Percy's *Reliques.* But it is to Hollinshed that Shakespeare is especially indebted, though it is probable he took hints and suggestions from an older play of the same name. The result, in the language of Edward Dowden, is " the greatest single achievement in poetry of the Teutonic or Northern genius." " It is," says Hazlitt, " the best of all Shakespeare's plays, for it is the one in which he was most in earnest. He was here fairly caught in the web of his own imagination."

LEAR, King of Britain, had three daughters: Goneril, wife to the Duke of Albany ; Regan, wife to the Duke of Cornwall; and Cordelia, a young maid, for whose love the King of France and Duke of Burgundy were joint suitors, and were at this time making stay for that purpose in the court of Lear.

The old king, worn out with age and the fatigues of government, he being more than fourscore years old, determined to take no further part in state affairs, but to leave the management[1] to younger strengths, that he might have time to prepare for death, which must at no long period ensue. With this intent he called his three daughters[2] to him, to know from their own lips which of them loved him best, that he might part his kingdom among them in such proportions as their affection for him should seem to deserve.

Goneril, the eldest, declared that she loved her father more than words could give out, that he was dearer to her than the light of her own eyes, dearer than life and liberty, with a deal of such professing stuff, which is easy to counterfeit where there is no real love, only a few fine words delivered with confidence being wanted in that case. The king, delighted to hear from her own mouth this assurance of her love, and thinking truly that her heart went with it, in a fit of fatherly fondness bestowed upon her and her husband one-third of his ample kingdom.

Then calling to him his second daughter, he demanded what she had to say. Regan, who was made of the same hollow metal as her sister, was not a whit behind in her professions, but rather declared that what her sister had spoken came short of the love which she professed to bear for his highness, insomuch that she found all other joys dead in comparison with the pleasure which she took in the love of her dear king and father. Lear blessed himself in having such loving children as he thought, and could do no less, after the handsome assurances which Regan had made, than bestow a third of his kingdom upon her and her husband equal in size to that which he had already given away to Goneril.

Then turning to his youngest daughter Cordelia, whom he called his joy, he asked what she had to say, thinking no doubt that she would glad his ears with the same loving speeches which her sisters had uttered, or rather that her expressions would be so much stronger than theirs, as she had always been his darling,

---

[1] **Leave the management.**—It would appear from the opening sentence of Act I. that Lear had at first intended to divide the kingdom equally among his children : and so much of his intention he had communicated to Kent and Gloucester. His "darker purpose" develops itself in the course of the scene.

[2] **Called his three daughters, etc.**—Read and quote this part of Act I., in which Lear's two wicked daughters profess their deep love for him, and the gentle Cordelia is discarded by the angry king.

and favored by him above either of them. But Cordelia, disgusted with the flattery of her sisters, whose hearts she knew were far from their lips, and seeing that all their coaxing speeches were only intended to wheedle the old king out of his dominions that they and their husbands might reign in his lifetime, made no other reply but this—that she loved his majesty according to her duty, neither more nor less. The king, shocked with this appearance of ingratitude in his favorite child, desired her to consider her words and to mend her speech, lest it should mar her fortunes. Cordelia then told her father [1] that he was her father, that he had given her breeding, and loved her; that she returned those duties back as was most fit, and did obey him, love him, and most honor him. But that she could not frame her mouth to such large speeches as her sisters had done, or promise to love nothing else in the world. Why had her sisters husbands, if (as they said) they had no love for anything but their father? If she should ever wed, she was sure the lord to whom she gave her hand would want half her love, half of her care and duty; she should never marry like her sisters, to love her father all.

Cordelia, who in earnest loved her old father even almost as extravagantly as her sisters pretended to do, would have plainly told him so at any other time in more daughter-like and loving terms, and without these qualifications, which did indeed sound a little ungracious; but after the crafty, flattering speeches of her sisters, which drew such extravagant rewards, she thought the handsomest thing she could do was to love and be silent. This put her affection out of suspicion of mercenary ends, and showed that she loved, but not for gain; and that her professions, the less ostentatious they were, had so much the more of truth and sincerity than her sisters.

This plainness of speech, which Lear called pride, so enraged the old monarch—who in his best of times always showed much of spleen and rashness, and in whom the dotage incident to old age

---

[1] **Told her father, etc.**—Read and quote the passage, Act I., Scene 1, beginning:—

  " Unhappy that I am, I cannot heave
  My heart into my heart."

had so clouded over his reason that he could not discern truth
from flattery, nor a gay painted speech from words that came
from the heart—that in a fury of resentment he retracted the
third part of his kingdom which he had reserved for Cordelia,
and gave it away from her, sharing it equally between her two
sisters and their husbands, the Dukes of Albany and Cornwall,
whom he now called to him, and in presence of all his courtiers,
bestowing a coronet between them, invested them jointly with
all the power, revenue, and execution of government, only
retaining to himself the name of king; all the rest of royalty he
resigned, with this reservation, that himself, with a hundred
knights for his attendants, was to be maintained in each of his
daughters' palaces in turn.

So preposterous a disposal of his kingdom, so little guided by
reason and so much by passion, filled all his courtiers with
astonishment and sorrow; but none of them had the courage to
interpose between this incensed king and his wrath except the
Earl of Kent,[1] who was beginning to speak a good word for
Cordelia, when the passionate Lear, on pain of death, commanded
him to desist; but the good Kent was not so to be repelled. He
had been ever loyal to Lear, whom he had honored as a king,
loved as a father, followed as a master; and had never esteemed
his life further than as a pawn to wage against his royal master's
enemies, nor feared to lose it when Lear's safety was the motive;
nor now that Lear was most his own enemy, did this faithful
servant of the king forget his old principles, but manfully
opposed Lear to do Lear good; and was unmannerly only because Lear was mad. He had been a most faithful counsellor in
times past to the king, and he besought him now that he would
see with his eyes (as he had done in many weighty matters), and
go by his advice still, and in his best consideration recall this
hideous rashness; for he would answer with his life, his judgment, that Lear's youngest daughter did not love him least, nor
were those empty-hearted whose low sound gave no token of

---

[1] **The Earl of Kent.**—Kent is, perhaps, the nearest to perfect goodness in
all Shakespeare's characters. There is an extraordinary charm in his bluntness.
His passionate affection for and fidelity to Lear act on our feelings in Lear's
own favor; virtue seems to be in company with him.—*Coleridge.*

hollowness. When power bowed to flattery, honor was bound
to plainness. For Lear's threats, what could he do to him, whose
life was already at his service? That should not hinder duty
from speaking.

The honest freedom of this good Earl of Kent only stirred up
the king's wrath the more; and like a frantic patient who kills
his physician and loves his mortal disease, he banished this true
servant, and allotted him but five days to make his preparations
for departure; but if on the sixth his hated person was found
within the realm of Britain, that moment was to be his death.
And Kent bade farewell to the king, and said, that since he
chose to show himself in such a fashion, it was but banishment
to stay there; and before he went, he recommended Cordelia to
the protection of the gods—the maid who had so rightly thought
and so discreetly spoken; and only wished that her sisters'
large speeches might be answered with deeds of love; and
then he went, as he said, to shape his old course to a new
country.

The King of France and Duke of Burgundy were now called
in to hear the determination of Lear about his youngest daughter,
and to know whether they would persist in their courtship to
Cordelia, now that she was under her father's displeasure, and
had no fortune but her own person to recommend her. The
Duke of Burgundy declined the match, and would not take her
to wife upon such conditions; but the King of France, under-
standing what the nature of the fault had been which had lost
her the love of her father, that it was only a tardiness of speech,
and the not being able to frame her tongue to flattery like her
sisters, took this young maid [1] by the hand, and saying that her
virtues were a dowry above a kingdom, bade Cordelia to take
farewell of her sisters and of her father, though he had been unkind; and she should go with him, and be queen of him and
of fair France, and reign over fairer possessions than her sisters;
and he called the Duke of Burgundy, in contempt, a waterish

---

[1] **Took this young maid.**—Read and quote the passage in which the King
of France invites Cordelia to be his queen, Act I., Scene 1, beginning:
"Fairest Cordelia, thou art most rich being poor,
Most choice forsaken, and most lov'd despis'd."

duke, because his love for this young maid had in a moment run all away like water.

Then Cordelia, with weeping eyes, took leave of her sisters, and besought them to love their father well and make good their professions; and they sullenly told her not to prescribe to them, for they knew their duty, but to strive to content her husband who had taken her (as they tauntingly expressed it) as Fortune's alms. And Cordelia with a heavy heart departed, for she knew the cunning of her sisters; and she wished her father in better hands than she was about to leave him in.

Cordelia was no sooner gone than the devilish dispositions of her sisters began to show themselves in their true colors. Even before the expiration of the first month, which Lear was to spend by agreement with his eldest daughter Goneril, the old king began to find out the difference between promises and performances. This wretch having got from her father all that he had to bestow, even to the giving away of the crown from off his head, began to grudge even those small remnants of royalty which the old man had reserved to himself, to please his fancy with the idea of being still a king. She could not bear to see him and his hundred knights. Every time she met her father, she put on a frowning countenance; and when the old man wanted to speak with her, she would feign sickness, or anything to be rid of the sight of him; for it was plain that she esteemed his old age a useless burden, and his attendants an unnecessary expense. Not only she herself slackened in her expressions of duty to the king, but by her example, and (it is to be feared) not without her private instructions, her very servants treated him with neglect, and would refuse to obey his orders, or still more contemptuously pretend not to hear him. Lear could not but perceive this alteration in the behavior of his daughter, but he shut his eyes against it as long as he could, as people commonly are unwilling to believe the unpleasant consequences which their own mistakes and obstinacy have brought upon them.

True love and fidelity are no more to be estranged by ill, than falsehood and hollow-heartedness can be conciliated by good usage. This eminently appears in the instance of the good Earl

of Kent, who, though banished by Lear, and his life made forfeit
if he were found in Britain, chose to stay and abide all consequences, as long as there was a chance of his being useful to
the king his master.   See to what mean shifts and disguises poor
loyalty is forced to submit sometimes ; yet it counts nothing base
or unworthy, so as it can but do service where it owes an obliga-
tion.   In the disguise of a serving-man, all his greatness and
pomp laid aside, this good earl proffered his services to the king,
who not knowing him to be Kent in that disguise, but pleased
with a certain plainness, or rather bluntness, in his answers which
the earl put on (so different from that smooth oily flattery which
he had so much reason to be sick of, having found the effects
not answerable in his daughter), a bargain was quickly struck,
and Lear took Kent into his service by the name of Caius, as he
called himself, never suspecting him to be his once great favorite, the high and mighty Earl of Kent.   This Caius quickly
found means to show his fidelity and love to his royal master ;
for Goneril's steward that same day behaving in a disrespectful
manner to Lear, and giving him saucy looks and language, as no
doubt he was secretly encouraged to do by his mistress, Caius,
not enduring to hear so open an affront put upon majesty, made
no more ado but presently tripped up his heels, and laid the
unmannerly slave in the kennel, for which friendly service Lear
became more and more attached to him.

Nor was Kent the only friend Lear had.   In his degree, and as
far as so insignificant a personage could show his love, the poor
fool,[1] or jester, that had been of his palace while Lear had a
palace, as it was the custom of kings and great personages at
that time to keep a fool (as he was called) to make them sport
after serious business; this poor fool clung to Lear after he had
given away his crown, and by his witty sayings would keep up
his good humor, though he could not refrain sometimes from
jeering at his master for his imprudence. in uncrowning himself,

---

[1] **Poor fool.**—In this tragedy the Fool rises to heroic proportions, as he
must have risen, to be in keeping with his surroundings. He has wisdom enough
to stock a college of philosophers,—wisdom which has come from long expe-
rience with the world without responsible relations to it. His whole soul is
bound up in his love for Lear and for Cordelia.—*Richard Grant White.*

and giving all away to his daughters; at which time, as he rhymingly expressed it, these daughters

> " For sudden joy did weep,
>   And he for sorrow sung,
> That such a king should play bo-peep,
>   And go the fools among."

And in such wild sayings and scraps of songs, of which he had plenty, this pleasant, honest fool poured out his heart even in the presence of Goneril herself, in many a bitter taunt and jest which cut to the quick; such as comparing the king to the hedge-sparrow, who feeds the young of the cuckoo till they grow old enough, and then has its head bit off for its pains; and saying, that an ass may know when the cart draws the horse (meaning that Lear's daughters, that ought to go behind, now ranked before their father); and that Lear was no longer Lear, but the shadow of Lear; for which free speeches he was once or twice threatened to be whipped.

The coolness and falling off of respect which Lear had begun to perceive, were not all which this foolish-fond father was to suffer from his unworthy daughter: she now plainly told him that his staying in her palace was inconvenient so long as he insisted upon keeping up an establishment of a hundred knights; and this establishment was useless and expensive, and only served to fill her court with riot and feasting; and she prayed him that he would lessen their number, and keep none but old men about him, such as himself, and fitting his age.

Lear at first could not believe his eyes or ears, nor that it was his daughter who spoke so unkindly. He could not believe that she who had received a crown from him should seek to cut off his train, and grudge him the respect due to his old age. But she persisting in her undutiful demand, the old man's rage was so excited, that he called her a detested kite, and said that she spoke an untruth: and so indeed she did, for the hundred knights were all men of choice behavior and sobriety of manners, skilled in all particulars of duty, and not given to rioting and feasting as she said. And he bid his horses to be prepared, for he would go to his other daughter, Regan, he and his hundred knights: and he spoke of ingratitude, and said it was a marble-hearted devil, and showed more hideous in a child than the sea-monster. And he cursed his eldest daughter [1] Goneril so as was terrible to hear: praying that she might never have a child, or if she had, that it might live to return that scorn and contempt upon her, which she had shown to him; that she might feel how sharper than a serpent's tooth it was to have a thankless child, and Goneril's husband, the Duke of Albany, beginning to excuse himself for any share which Lear might suppose he had in the unkindness, Lear would not hear him out, but in a rage ordered his horses to be saddled, and set out with his followers for the abode of Regan, his other daughter. And Lear thought to himself, how small the fault of Cordelia, (if it was a fault) now appeared, in comparison with her sister's, and he wept; and then he was ashamed that such a creature as Goneril should have so much power over his manhood as to make him weep.

Regan and her husband were keeping their court in great pomp and state at their palace; and Lear dispatched his servant Caius with letters to his daughter, that she might be prepared for his reception, while he and his train followed after. But it seems that Goneril had been beforehand with him, sending letters also to Regan, accusing her father with waywardness and ill-humors, and advising her not to receive so great a train as he was bringing with him. This messenger arrived at the same time with Caius, and Caius and he met; and who should it be but Caius' old enemy the steward, whom he had formerly tripped up by the heels for his saucy behavior to Lear. Caius not liking the fellow's look, and suspecting what he came for, began to revile him, and challenged him to fight, which the fellow refusing, Caius, in a fit of honest passion, beat him soundly, as such a mischief-maker and carrier of wicked messages deserved: which coming to the ears of Regan and her husband, they ordered Caius to be put in the stocks, though he was a messenger from the king her father, and in that character demanded the highest respect; so that the first thing the king

---

[1] **Cursed his eldest daughter.**—The language in the text is too scathing for pleasant reading. A critic remarks that we shall have to go to the Book of Deuteronomy to find a parallel for the concentrated force of this curse.

saw when he entered the castle, was his faithful servant Caius sitting in that disgraceful situation.

This was but a bad omen of the reception which he was to expect; but a worse followed, when upon inquiry for his daughter and her husband, he was told they were weary with traveling all night, and could not see him: and when lastly, upon his insisting in a positive and angry manner to see them, they came to greet him, whom should he see in their company but the hated Goneril, who had come to tell her own story, and set her sister against the king her father!

This sight much moved the old man, and still more to see Regan take her by the hand: and he asked Goneril if she was not ashamed to look upon his white beard? And Regan advised him to go home again with Goneril, and live with her peaceably, dismissing half of his attendants, and to ask her forgiveness; for he was old and wanted discretion, and must be ruled and led by persons that had more discretion than himself. And Lear showed how preposterous that would sound, if he were to go down on his knees, and beg of his own daughter for food and raiment, and he argued against such an unnatural dependence; declaring his resolution never to return with her, but to stay where he was with Regan, he and his hundred knights: for he said that she had not forgot the half of the kingdom which he had endowed her with, and that her eyes were not fierce like Goneril's, but mild and kind. And he said that rather than return to Goneril, with half his train cut off, he would go over to France, and beg a wretched pension of the king there, who had married his youngest daughter without a portion.

But he was mistaken in expecting kinder treatment of Regan than he had experienced from her sister Goneril. As if willing to outdo her sister in unfilial behavior, she declared that she thought fifty knights too many to wait upon him—that five-and-twenty were enough. Then Lear, nigh heart-broken, turned to Goneril, and said that he would go back with her, for her fifty doubled five-and-twenty, and so her love was twice as much as Regan's. But Goneril excused herself, and said, "What need of so many as five-and-twenty? or even ten? or five? when he might be waited upon by her servants or her sister's servants?

So these two wicked daughters, as if they strove to exceed each other in cruelty to their old father who had been so good to them, by little and little would have abated him of all his train, all respect (little enough for him that once commanded a kingdom), which was left him to show that he had once been a king! Not that a splendid train is essential to happiness, but from a king to a beggar is a hard change, from commanding millions to be without one attendant; and it was the ingratitude in his daughters denying it, more than what he would suffer by the want of it, which pierced this poor king to the heart: insomuch that with this double ill-usage, and vexation for having so foolishly given away a kingdom, his wits began to be unsettled, and while he said he knew not what, he vowed revenge against those unnatural hags, and to make examples of them that should be a terror to the earth!

While he was thus idly threatening what his weak arm could never execute, night came on, and a loud storm of thunder and lightning with rain; and his daughters still persisting in their resolution not to admit his followers, he called for his horses, and chose rather to encounter the utmost fury of the storm abroad, than stay under the same roof with these ungrateful daughters: and they, saying that the injuries which wilful men procure to themselves, are their just punishment, suffered him to go in that condition, and shut their doors upon him.

The winds were high, and the rain and storm increased, when the old man sallied forth to combat with the elements, less sharp than his daughters' unkindness. For many miles about there was scarce a bush; and there upon a heath, exposed to the fury of the storm in a dark night, did King Lear wander out, and defy the winds and the thunder: and he bid the winds [1] to blow the earth into the sea, or swell the waves of the sea, till they drowned the earth, that no token might remain of any such ungrateful animal as man. The old king was now left with no companion but the poor fool, who still abided with him, with his

---

[1] **Bid the winds.**—Read and quote this great passage of the play, in which Lear and the Fool are exposed to the fury of the tempest, Act III., Scenes 2 and 4, beginning :—
" Blow, winds, and crack your cheeks !" etc.

merry conceits striving to out-jest misfortune, saying, it was but
a naughty night to swim in, and truly the king had better go in
and ask his daughter's blessing:

> " But he that has a little tiny wit,
>   With heigh ho, the wind and rain !
>   Must make content with his fortunes fit,
>   Though the rain it raineth every day: "

and swearing it was a brave night to cool a lady's pride.

Thus poorly accompanied, this once great monarch was found
by his ever faithful servant the good Earl of Kent, now trans-
formed to Caius, who ever followed close at his side, though the
king did not know him to be the earl; and he said, "Alas! sir,
are you here? Creatures that love night love not such nights as
these. This dreadful storm has driven the beasts to their hiding-
places. Man's nature cannot endure the affliction or the fear."
And Lear rebuked him, and said, these lesser evils were not felt,
where a greater malady was fixed. When the mind is at ease,
the body has leisure to be delicate; but the tempest in his mind
did take all feelings else from his senses, but of that which beat
at his heart. And he spoke of filial ingratitude, and said it was
all one as if the mouth should tear the hand for lifting food to
it; for parents were hands and food and everything to children.

But the good Caius still persisting in his entreaties that the
king would not stay out in the open air, at last persuaded him
to enter a little wretched hovel which stood upon the heath,
where the fool first entering, suddenly ran back terrified, saying
that he had seen a spirit. But upon examination this spirit
proved to be nothing more than a poor Bedlam-beggar, who had
crept into this deserted hovel for shelter, and with his talk
about devils frightened the fool, one of those poor lunatics who
are either mad, or feign to be so, the better to extort charity from
the compassionate country-people; who go about the country
calling themselves poor Tom and poor Turlygood, saying, "Who
gives anything to poor Tom?" sticking pins and nails and
sprigs of rosemary into their arms to make them bleed; with
such horrible actions, partly by prayers, and partly with lunatic
curses, they move or terrify the ignorant country folks into
giving them alms. This poor fellow was such a one; and the

king seeing him in so wretched a plight, with nothing but a blanket about his loins to cover his nakedness, could not be persuaded but that the fellow was some father who had given all away to his daughters, and brought himself to that pass; for nothing, he thought, could bring a man to such wretchedness but the having unkind daughters.

And from this and many such wild speeches which he uttered, the good Caius plainly perceived that he was not in his perfect mind, but that his daughters' ill-usage had really made him go mad.[1] And now the loyalty of this worthy Earl of Kent showed itself in more essential services than he had hitherto found opportunity to perform. For with the assistance of some of the king's attendants who remained loyal, he had the person of his royal master removed at daybreak to the castle of Dover, where his own friends and influence, as Earl of Kent, chiefly lay; and himself embarking for France, hastened to the court of Cordelia, and did there in such moving terms represent the pitiful condition of her royal father, and set out in such lively colors the inhumanity of her sisters; that this good and loving child with many tears besought the king her husband, that he would give her leave to embark for England with a sufficient power to subdue these cruel daughters and their husbands, and restore the old king, her father, to his throne; which being granted, she set forth, and with a royal army she landed at Dover.

Lear having by some chance escaped from the guardians which the good Earl of Kent had put over him to take care of him in his lunacy, was found by some of Cordelia's train, wandering about the fields near Dover, in a pitiable condition, stark mad and singing aloud to himself, with a crown upon his head which he had made of straw and nettles, and other wild weeds that he had picked up in the corn fields. By the advice of the physicians, Cordelia, though earnestly desirous of seeing her father, was prevailed upon to put off the meeting, till by sleep

---

[1] **Made him go mad.**—Dr. Bucknill remarks: "Insanity arising from mental and moral causes often continues in a certain state of imperfect development; . . . . . a state of exaggerated and perverted emotion, accompanied by violent and irregular conduct, but unconnected with intellectual aberration; until some physical shock is incurred,—bodily illness, or accident, or exposure to physical suffering; and then the imperfect type of mental disease is converted into perfect lunacy, characterized by a more or less profound affection of the intellect, by delusion or incoherence."

and the operation of herbs which they gave him, he should be restored to greater composure. By the aid of these skilful physicians, to whom Cordelia promised all her gold and jewels for the recovery of the old king, Lear was soon in a condition to see his daughter.

A tender sight it was to see the meeting between this father and daughter;[1] to see the struggles between the joy of this poor old king at beholding again his once darling child, and the shame at receiving such filial kindess from her whom he had cast off for so small a fault in his displeasure; both these passions struggling with the remains of his malady, which, in his half-crazed brain, sometimes made him that he scarce remembered where he was, or who it was that so kindly kissed him and spoke to him; and then he would beg the standers-by not to laugh at him if he were mistaken in thinking this lady to be his daughter Cordelia! And then to see him fall on his knees to beg pardon of his child; and she, good lady, kneeling all the while to ask a blessing of him, and telling him that it did not become him to kneel, but it was her duty, for she was his child—his true and very child Cordelia! And she kissed him (as she said) to kiss away all her sisters' unkindness, and said that they might be ashamed of themselves to turn their old kind father with his white beard out into the cold air, when her enemy's dog, though it had bit her (as she prettily expressed it), should have stayed by her fire such a night as that and warmed himself. And she told her father how she had come from France with purpose to bring him assistance; and he said that she must forget and forgive, for he was old and foolish and did not know what he did, but that to be sure she had great cause not to love him, but her sisters had none. And Cordelia said that she had no cause, no more than they had. So we will leave this old king in the protection of this dutiful and loving child, where by the help of sleep[2] and

---

[1] **Meeting between father and daughter.**—Read and quote the touch-ing scene in which Cordelia meets her father, Act IV., Scene 7, beginning:—
" O thou good Kent, how shall I live and work," etc.

[2] **Help of sleep, etc.**—One wonders at Shakespeare's profound knowledge of mental disease. Although, nearly two hundred and fifty years have passed since the Great Dramatist thus wrote, science has very little to add to the method of treating the insane as set forth in *Lear*.

medicine, she and her physicians at length succeeded in winding up the untuned and jarring senses which the cruelty of his other daughters had so violently shaken. Let us return to say a word or two about those cruel daughters.

These monsters of ingratitude, who had been so false to their old father, could not be expected to prove more faithful to their own husbands. They soon grew tired of paying even the appearance of duty and affection, and in an open way showed that they had fixed their loves upon another. It happened that the object of their guilty loves was the same. It was Edmund, a natural son of the late Earl of Gloucester, who, by his treacheries, had succeeded in disinheriting his brother Edgar, the lawful heir, from his earldom, and by his wicked practices was now earl himself —a wicked man, and a fit object for the love of such wicked creatures as Goneril and Regan. It falling out about this time that the Duke of Cornwall, Regan's husband, died, Regan immediately declared her intention of wedding this Earl of Gloucester, which roused the jealousy of her sister—to whom as well as to Regan this wicked earl had at sundry times professed love —Goneril found means to make away with her sister by poison; but being detected in her practices, and imprisoned by her husband, the Duke of Albany, for this deed, and for her guilty passion for the earl, which had come to his ears, she, in a fit of disappointed love and rage, shortly put an end to her own life. Thus the justice of Heaven at last overtook these wicked daughters.

While the eyes of all men were upon this event, admiring the justice displayed in their deserved deaths, the same eyes were suddenly taken off from this sight to admire at the mysterious ways of the same power in the melancholy fate of the young and virtuous daughter, the lady Cordelia, whose good deeds did seem to deserve a more fortunate conclusion; but it is an awful truth that innocence and piety are not always successful in this world. The forces which Goneril and Regan had sent out under the command of the bad Earl of Gloucester were victorious; and Cordelia, by the practices of this wicked earl—who did not like that any should stand between him and the throne—ended her

9 781340 477134